Yes, I Can!

The story of the Jamaican Bobsled Team

by Devon Harris

illustrated by Ricardo Cortés

For information regarding permission, write to:
Waterhouse Publishing, 40 Sheridan Ave, Congers, NY 10920

ISBN: 0-9764082-5-2

Library of Congress Control Number: 2007932449

1. Bobsledding—Jamaica—Biography—Juvenile Literature
2. Olympics Games (15th: 1988: Calgary, Canada) Juvenile Literature

Printed in China

www.devonharrislive.com

To my children Devon, Yanitza, Brandon and Summer.

Always believe in yourself and know that it is true,
when you set your mind to it there is nothing you can't do.

Yes, I Can!

People in many faraway lands
Were surprised and could not understand
Why several Jamaicans would dare to dream
Of starting their own bobsled team.
"That's impossible! Is it not?
Jamaica," they said, "is just too hot.
And on an island where it often rains,
How in the world would they ever train?
You're from the sunny Caribbean;
Forget about being a Winter Olympian."

There were lots of jokes, teasing and laughter

About the boys from the land of wood and water.

Few words were kind; people mocked instead,

And with one loud voice they negatively said,

"Stick to the sun, the sand and the beach;

The Olympics you could never reach.

Spare yourselves and take our advice:

Tropical boys don't belong on ice.

And in case you somehow don't remember:

We're already in the month of September!

So how could you be ready by February

To compete in the Olympics in Calgary?"

But Devon, Michael, Dudley and Chris
Truly believed they could accomplish this.
They firmly joined their hearts and hands,
And with one voice shouted, "Yes, I Can!"
Dudley Stokes' favorite sport was soccer.
Chris, Dudley's brother, was a sprinter.
Michael White was also a sprinter – the fastest.
Devon Harris was a runner – and the strongest.
Refusing to listen to either mockery or jest,
They put all their heart in their bobsled quest.
And from their sports, they brought to bear
The skills they would need for their bold new dare.

In Jamaica where the weather is usually nice,
Far from any mountains with snow and ice,
They had no helmets to protect their heads
While riding on a makeshift sled.
For many hours in the boiling sun,
They worked very hard to get it done –
Lifting weights, pushing and running,
Preparing themselves for something stunning.

Then to Lake Placid, New York, to meet their coach –
The very thing they needed most.
An accomplished bobsledder, a former Olympian,
Taking on the challenge to train four green Jamaicans.
He said, "Bobsledding is a sport of speed,
But there are other things that you will need:
Strong motivation, goals with clarity,
And a belief that greatness is your destiny.
Listen to the things that I will teach
And to the Olympics you will surely reach."

The American team members also did their part,
Teaching the Jamaicans the bobsled start.
But they continued to fall on the hard ice rink;
Some people laughed, saying, "It's harder than you think."
For the first time in Lake Placid, they saw a bobsled track:
The huge sloping turns left them in shock.
The intimidating walls of bare concrete
Stood in the air almost twenty-five feet!
Yes, looking at the track gave them a frightening chill
As they thought of themselves racing down the hill.

They worked very hard even though they were fearful
That their efforts to the Olympics might not be successful.
An important lesson they clearly taught:
Life's road is rocky, and you're often caught
With challenges and obstacles that will cause you to fear;
But act with courage, and your goals will draw near.
So whenever you find yourself in a jam,
Whisper to yourself, "Yes, I Can!"

Bobsledding was difficult as they were often told,
And the temperatures were low and bitterly cold.
But to their credit, they stuck to their dream
And with much cooperation worked together as a team.
Encouraging and scolding, challenging each other,
Each one helped the other to go even further.
And even though they sometimes drove each other berserk,
They succeeded because they focused on teamwork.

Dudley was the driver; the others were pushers.
Together the four of them supplied the power,
Sitting on their egos and embracing their roles,
Doing all they could to achieve their goals.
They said, "No man is an island, although we're from one;
We will finish this journey, the way it had begun.
We will believe in each other, through the bad times and good,
And support each other in the way that we should."

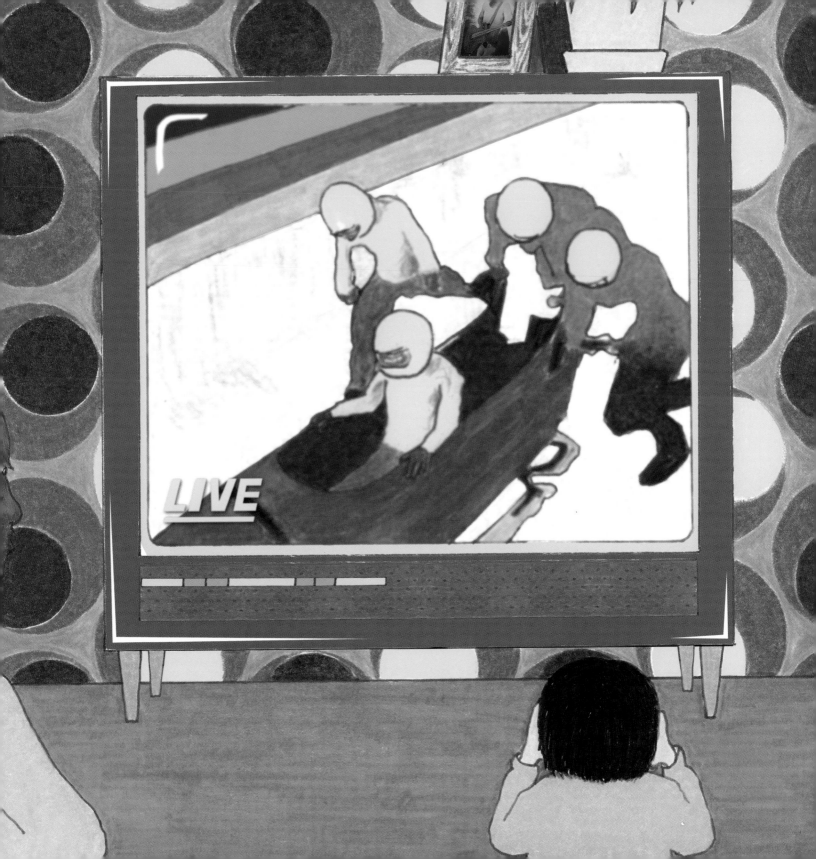

Television cameras from all over the world

Made sure their incredible story was told.

And oh, people laughed, had lots of frolic and fun

About the bobsledders from the land of sea and sun.

But they were fearless in their quest for glory;

Their unwavering tenacity became the strength of their story.

So never give up when the going gets tough,

Filled with disappointments, frustrations and such.

Dig in your heels like the unconquerable man;

Look straight in the mirror and say, "Yes, I Can!"

The Canadians, Italians, Swiss and Germans

Had a superb history and a fine bobsled tradition.

Going to the Olympics, I'm sure you can guess,

They had sleds and equipment that were the best.

But the Jamaicans who were not as established yet,

Had to make do on a very tight budget.

Every night before retiring to bed,

They thought of ways to buy a good sled.

No fancy uniforms – Oh what a sight!

But they kept on going despite their plight.

They said, "If we unite our minds, there's no doubt we'll find

A definite way to get through this grind."

The T-shirts they made looked really nice,
Declaring themselves *"The Hottest Thing on Ice."*
The money they raised paid for rooms that were cheap,
With some left over to buy food to eat.
Their determination was rewarded by sponsors and gifts
From friends and well-wishers who made them a hit.
And soon they had more than enough it would seem
To become the first Jamaicans on a Winter Olympic Team.
So when your way seems as dark as midnight,
Don't you give in – put up a fight.
Believe in yourself like the invincible man;
Hold your chin up, and say, "Yes, I Can!"

It was a great day in Olympic history
To see them march in the opening ceremony.
How they were proud and how they were glad
To see the black, green and gold: the colors of their flag.
Leading their delegation in the parade of nations,
They smiled and waved to standing ovations.
Dudley was the captain, so he led the way;
Behind were Devon, Michael and Chris – kings that day.
Freddy Powell and Caswell Allen strolled gaily in the back;
If anyone got injured, they were ready to take the track.
Everyone was happy that they had persevered
And so in their success they jubilantly shared.

They all felt great, as well as they should,
Thinking of the times that they very well could
Have turned away from following their dream
Of being Jamaica's first bobsled team.
They said, "On the road of life, there are many twists and turns
And the sting of others who ridicule and spurn.
But the success and respect that together we know
Came because we kept focused and never let go."

The Olympic Village was a really neat place
Where they met countless people of all color and race:
Coming together in a world community;
Living in love, peace and harmony;
Exchanging pins and taking photos;
Hanging out at the diner with French fries and burgers.
There was even a discotheque and game arcade –
When they were in the village, they had it made.
But the Olympic Village was a serious place too,
For in the back of their minds they always knew
They were there to compete and be at their best,
So they went to bed early to get plenty of rest.

"Unforgettable!" is what many would say
To see the Jamaicans appear on race day.
The crowd fell silent for a little while
As they got ready to bobsled, Jamaican style.
Like the great Jackie Robinson of the Brooklyn Dodgers,
The dream of Martin Luther King and many others,
They stood at the start of not just a race,
But the doorway to history with poise and grace.
Those greats had dreamt and paved the way
For Jamaica to compete in Calgary that day.

With a shiny sled painted black, gold and green,

And brand new uniforms with a sensational sheen,

The excitement was high, and the crowd very loud,

As they stood at the start – ready and proud.

The time had arrived; the track was clear for them to go,

And they got themselves ready to put on a show.

Feet on the starting blocks, hands on the push bar,

The same look of determination that had brought them so far.

Ready! Set! Go! – Oh, how fast they ran,

Saying to themselves, "Yes, I Can!"

In about ten seconds they were all in the sled,
Dudley looking forward, the others bowing their heads.
Devon was behind Dudley, sledder number two,
Followed by Michael and Chris, the rest of the crew.
They were filled with excitement, felt the pounding of their hearts
As they heard someone say, "They had one of the fastest starts."

The sled trickled slowly through the first few turns
And then sped up so quickly your stomach would churn.
Like a roller coaster it went round and round,
Twisting and turning really close to the ground.
They had gained so much speed by the end of turn five –
You would never go so fast in a car when you drive.

Through turn six and seven, screaming through turn eight,
They were on top of the world, everything was great.
At the tip of turn nine, came the end of the line;
They felt their bodies move slowly, suspended in time.
The sled flipped over and they crashed on their heads!
It was so spectacular, everyone thought they were dead.
The sled whipped around the corners in such a fierce way
That it still looks scary when you see it today.

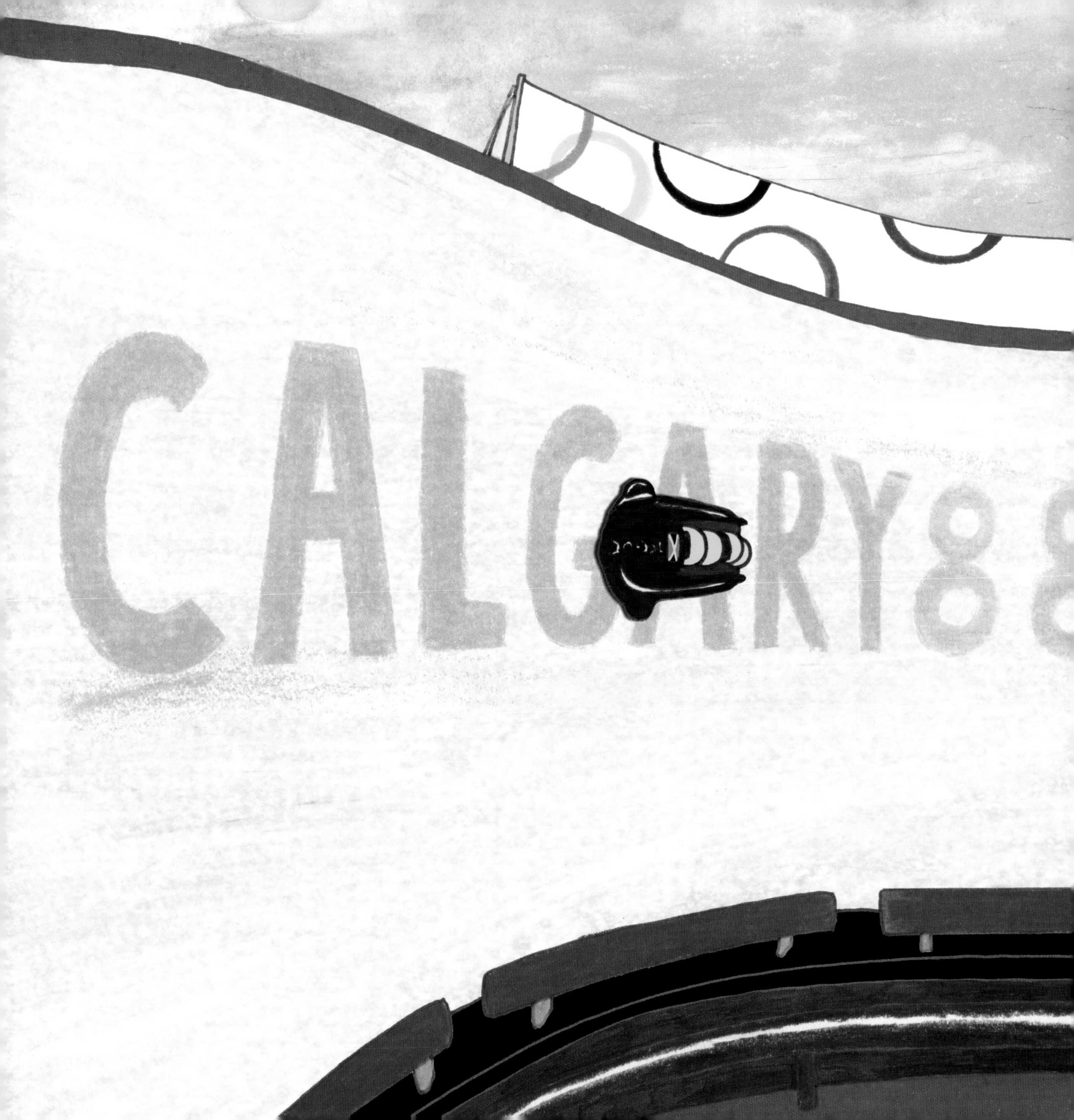
CALGARY88

Inside the sled was frightening, to say the very least,

As they rattled and rolled inside the wrecked beast.

Slamming their heads against the tall icy walls,

They felt like Humpty Dumpy, who had a great fall.

Flashes of white flew past their eyes,

The bottom of the sled scraping the skies.

The burning of the fiberglass was an awful smell,

A frightening experience, I'm sure you can tell.

As the sled slammed down the track upon its side,
Their self-esteem sank, their confidence nearly died.
The whole world would say that the Jamaicans had failed,
And they could feel their courage begin to sink and bail.
All kinds of thoughts flooded through their heads,
Especially the fears that great dreamers dread:
What about the little boy sitting at home,
Facing his demons, his fears all alone?
What about the girl who is always sad in gym,
The last one to be chosen because the others want to win?

What about the underdogs all over the world?
Who because they are different, they are oftentimes told,
"Stand on the sidelines; you are truly outclassed.
You could never succeed; you're not up to the task."
It is for them the greats have fought and won.
And with them, that day, the Jamaicans marched as one.
They said, "We may not have achieved our desired outcome,
But until we cross the finish line, the work is not done.
So let's gather up our strength one more time,
And push the sled across the finish line."

They walked to the finish with their heads hanging down,
Their usual bright smiles replaced by a frown.
The crowd said, "We love you. We love you. Look up. Be proud.
Tell the world you've succeeded, and shout it out loud.
You didn't get a medal, but indeed you've won
Our hearts and appreciation for what you've done.
You have shown us that through hard work and determination,
We can achieve the things in our imagination."

Another important lesson from the Jamaicans we can learn:

Success isn't always measured in the results that you earn.

Even if you didn't score high on your test,

Be content in knowing you did your very best.

So all of you kids who are in school,

Enjoy your lessons, for learning is cool.

And even when the work gets too hard, it seems,

Never forget to follow your dreams.

Do this always and know that it's true:

When you set your mind to it, there's nothing you can't do.

Be like the bobsledders who were Jamaicans;

Believe in yourself and say, "Yes I Can!"

HISTORY OF BOBSLEDDING

Believe it or not, bobsledding did not start in Jamaica. The sport started in Albany, New York around 1897. It quickly migrated to Switzerland and caught on with American and British tourists, spurring interest throughout Europe.

The first racing sleds were made of wood, but were soon replaced by faster, smoother steel sleds. On these sleeker models, competitors "bobbed" back and forth to increase their speed on the straight ways. From this motion came the name bobsledding. The best sledders soon realized the bobbing didn't increase speed. Still, the name stuck.

On January 5, 1898, the Cresta Run in St. Moritz, Switzerland hosted the first organized bobsled competition. The sled held five-passengers, thee men and two women. For better steering, the sleds were equipped with four runners, positioned on axles much like the four wheels of a car. With the new design, speeds on the mountainside became dangerously fast. For safety purposes, an artificial bobsled run with a gentler slope was built in St. Moritz in 1902.

It took about twenty years for bobsledding to become a widely accepted sport. Once it caught on, the excitement of bobsledding attracted athletes from other sports that required speed, grace and courage. Competitors from track and field, handball, basketball, American football and gymnastics contributed to the development of the most important part of bobsled racing – an explosive push at the start. Today the world's top teams train year round and, compete on artificial ice tracks in swift modern sleds, made of fiberglass and steel.

The U. S. dominated Olympic bobsledding until 1952, when they failed to win gold in both bobsledding events, managing to take only the silver. Since that landmark year European countries, especially Switzerland and Germany, have been the frontrunners in international competition. The Swiss have won more medals in Olympic, World and European championships and World Cup competitions than any other nation.

Bolstered by new sled design and construction, East Germany became a major player in the mid 1970s. The reunified German team has continued to further advance the sport. Canada, Italy and Austria consistently give the Germans and Swiss a run for their money.

It wasn't until the 1990s that female bobsledders returned to the sport. When they did, they came on strong in both Europe and North America. Their daring and skill compelled the Olympic committee to add Women's Bobsledding to the competition in 2002. By all estimations, they're in for the long run.

Bobsledding has come a long way since 1897. It has spread from Albany, NY to nations as remote as Japan, Australia, New Zealand, and, of course Jamaica. New teams and superb athletes are pushing the century old sport to greater heights and faster speeds. With the arrival of cutting edge artificial tracks in Nagano, Japan, Park City, Utah, and Vancouver, British Columbia, bobsled racing promises to accelerate its run into a thrilling future.

Jamaica AT A GLANCE

Official Name: Jamaica. It is derived from the word Xaymaca which is the name given to the island by its original inhabitants, the Arawak Indians. Xaymaca means either the "Land of Springs," or the "Land of Wood and Water."

Capital City: Kingston, designated as the capital in 1872. It is also the largest city with a population of 937,700. Montego Bay is Jamaica's second largest city.

Population: 2.7 million. **Ethnic Groups:** 90% of Jamaicans are of West African descent; Mixed 7.3%; East Indian 1.3%; Chinese 0.2%; White 0.2%; and Other 0.1%.

Location: Almost at the centre of the Caribbean Sea. 18° north and 78° west.

Closest neighbors: Cuba is 90 miles south and Haiti is 100 miles west. **Closest point in the Americas:** Cartagena, Colombia is 445 miles almost due south. Miami is 571 miles from Kingston.

Climate: Tropical. Hot, humid, temperate interior.

Average Rainfall: 78 inches annually.

Size: With an area of 4,411 square miles, Jamaica is the largest English speaking island in the Caribbean and is slightly smaller than the state of Connecticut in the United States.

Length: 146 miles from east to west. **Width:** Its greatest width is 51 miles, from St. Ann's Bay to Portland Point.

Highest Point: The center of the island is mountainous with the highest point being the Blue Mountain Peak at 7,402 feet.

Lowest Point: The Caribbean Sea at sea level.

Traditional Olympic Sports: Badminton, Boxing, Cycling, Sailing, Shooting, Table Tennis, Track and Field, and Weightlifting.

FOOD FOR THOUGHT

1. Identify Jamaica, Lake Placid and Calgary on the map by pointing to each one.

2. Calgary and Lake Placid are both located in North America. Jamaica is in the Caribbean. Describe the differences in the climate of each place.

3. Explain why it never snows in Jamaica.

4. What sports do you think would normally be played in such a climate?

5. How did the team prepare in Jamaica to become Olympic Bobsledders?

6. Describe the challenges the team faced in Jamaica while preparing for the Winter Olympics.

7. How did the previous experience and funding of the Jamaican team compare with that of the other teams?

8. What skills would the team members have used from their original sports to help them in bobsledding?

9. What evidence can you list to support the view that the other teams were far better prepared than the Jamaicans?

10. Despite crashing during their run the Jamaican bobsled team was a huge success. What evidence supports that idea?

11. The Jamaicans believed in themselves. How does a strong belief in yourself help you to achieve your goals?

12. The Jamaicans focused on teamwork. What does it mean to be part of a team? How does being part of a team help you to achieve your goals?

ABOUT THE AUTHOR

Born on Christmas Day, 1964 and raised in the most notorious enclave of Olympic Gardens in Kingston, known as Waterhouse; the greatest gift Devon Harris ever received was the belief that a positive attitude and a never say die philosophy would carry him farther than a sense of injustice and a heart filled with anger. His early education at the Drews Avenue Primary School and Ardenne High School prepared him well for an appointment to the officer corps of the Jamaica Defence Force.

A graduate of the prestigious Royal Military Academy Sandhurst in England, Devon received a Queen's Commission in December 1985 and served in the officer corps of the Jamaica Defence Force until December 1992 when he retired as a Captain.

Encouraged by his commanding officer, Devon tried out for and was selected as a member of the Jamaica's first bobsled team which competed in Calgary, Canada in 1988. The Disney blockbuster movie *Cool Runnings* was based on them. Devon also competed in the 1992 Winter Olympic Games in Albertville, France and the 1998 Games in Nagano, Japan.

Presently, Devon is involved in a number of not-for profit organizations which support children around the world.

Keep on Pushing Foundation: As its founder, Devon aims to bring hope to youths in disadvantaged communities around the globe, by creating opportunities for them to explore their full potential.

Right to Play: As an athlete ambassador, Devon supports Right to Play's efforts in using sports and play in refugee camps to enhance child development and build community capacity.

Devon is married with four children, resides in New York and travels internationally as a Motivational Speaker, offering a captivating message of inspiration and hope.

Yes, I Can! is his first book.